PRECIOUS
MOMENTS

Blessed
Beginnings

————————————

GIVEN TO

————————————

OCCASION

————————————

DATE

> "Before I formed you in the womb I knew you;
> before you were born I sanctified you."
>
> Jeremiah 1:5

Before her little fingers curled around theirs . . . before his toothless grin ever touched their heart, they loved this precious gift from God. For so long, the two had dreamed of the day when all the plans, all the preparations would end and a precious new life would begin. Now the time has come, and changed their world forever. *Blessed Beginnings* captures the heart of this moment with the innocence and beauty only Sam Butcher's beloved characters can create. Alongside these heartwarming illustrations are special scriptures, selected to show another Father's love for His children—a love from heaven formed long before the world even began. Together the pictures and verses testify to the special bond between parent and child, God and His people—a beautiful reminder that God loves us as His very own.

Jesus said, "Let the little children come to Me, and do not forbid them; for of such is the kingdom of heaven."

Matthew 19:14

Behold, children are
a heritage from the LORD,
The fruit of the womb is a reward.
Like arrows in the
hand of a warrior,
So are the children
of one's youth.

Psalm 127:3–4

For this child I prayed,
and the LORD has granted me
my petition which I asked of Him.
Therefore I also have lent him
to the LORD; as long as he lives
he shall be lent to the LORD.

1 Samuel 1:27-28

Before I formed you in the womb I knew you; Before you were born I sanctified you.

Jeremiah 1:5

For You formed my inward parts;
You covered me in my
mother's womb.
I will praise You, for I am
fearfully and wonderfully made;
Marvelous are Your works,
And that my soul knows very well.

Psalm 139:13–14

By You I have
been upheld from birth;
You are He who took me out
of my mother's womb,
My praise shall
be continually of You.

Psalm 71:6

When you lie down,
you will not be afraid;
Yes, you will lie down
and your sleep
will be sweet.

Proverbs 3:24

For He shall give
His angels charge

over you,
To keep you in all

your ways.

Psalm 91:11

Out of the mouth of babes
and nursing infants
You have ordained
strength.

Psalm 8:2

Even a child is
known by his deeds,
Whether what he does
is pure and right.

Proverbs 20:11

My son, keep your father's command,
And do not forsake the law
of your mother. . . .
When you roam, they will lead you;
When you sleep, they will keep you;
And when you awake,
they will speak with you.

Proverbs 6:20, 22

All your children shall
be taught by the LORD,
And great shall be the
peace of your children.

Isaiah 54:13

Oh, that men would give thanks to the LORD for His goodness,
And for His wonderful works to the children of men!

Psalm 107:8

"Assuredly, I say to you,
unless you are converted
and become as little children,
you will by no means enter
the kingdom of heaven."

Matthew 18:3

> "For He shall give His angels charge over you,
> to keep you in all your ways."
>
> Psalm 91:11

How can someone so small fill your heart so completely? And how can you ever express the joy you feel each time you kiss those pudgy cheeks? We can celebrate the gift by looking to the Giver, remembering that all good things come from our Father above. As you enjoy the pastel pictures of baby's early days and read the Scriptures of God's heart for you and your children, remember that He, too, delights in your presence. In your crawling into His lap for protection, love, nourishment, and enjoyment, know that the same love you feel for your child, God feels for you. May this book help you to remember these precious days with your child, and grow ever closer to your own Father's love.